Fun Holiday Crafts
Kids Can Do!

Earth Day Crafts

Carol Gnojewski

EARTH DAY BOOK

Enslow Elementary
an imprint of

E **Enslow Publishers, Inc.**

40 Industrial Road   PO Box 38
Box 398   Aldershot
Berkeley Heights, NJ 07922   Hants GU12 6BP
USA   UK

http://www.enslow.com

Enslow Elementary, an imprint of Enslow Publishers, Inc.

Enslow Elementary® is a registered trademark of Enslow Publishers, Inc.

Library of Congress Cataloging-in-Publication Data

Gnojewski, Carol.
   Earth Day crafts / Carol Gnojewski.
      p. cm. — (Fun holiday crafts kids can do)
   Includes bibliographical references and index.
   ISBN 0-7660-2346-X
   1. Holiday decorations—Juvenile literature. 2. Handicraft—Juvenile literature.
3. Earth Day—Juvenile literature. I. Title. II. Series.
TT900.H6G59 2004
745.594'162—dc22   2004009623

Printed in the United States of America

10 9 8 7 6 5 4 3 2

To Our Readers: We have done our best to make sure all Internet Addresses in this book were active and appropriate when we went to press. However, the author and the publisher have no control over and assume no liability for the material available on those Internet sites or on other Web sites they may link to. Any comments or suggestions can be sent by e-mail to comments@enslow.com or to the address on the back cover.

Illustration Credits: Crafts prepared by June Ponte. Skjold Photographs, p. 4.
Photography by Carl Feryok.

Cover Illustration: Carl Feryok

Contents

Safety Note: Be sure to ask for help from an adult, if
needed, to complete these crafts!

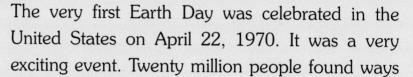

introduction

The very first Earth Day was celebrated in the United States on April 22, 1970. It was a very exciting event. Twenty million people found ways to show their concern about the earth. Ten thousand people met at the Washington Monument in Washington, D.C., to hear speeches and live music. Cities across the nation organized marches, cleanups, and recycling events. Schools scheduled field trips to clean up parks, beaches, and wilderness areas.

Recycling is one way that we can all reduce the amount of garbage that we produce.

The idea for Earth Day came from former Wisconsin senator Gaylord Nelson. He wanted to set aside a special day for Americans to teach each other about the problems that our planet is facing. With the help of a student named Denis Hayes, he gathered support for the holiday. They chose a date near the beginning of spring when people traditionally honor the new planting year. Since there are no other holidays at this time, schools, colleges, and businesses could all participate. They wanted everyone to join in the Earth Day festivities!

Earth Day was not celebrated again until 1990. It was an international event. People all over the world took part in it. Now it is celebrated every year around the world. It is a day for awareness, problem solving, and action. But the work done on Earth Day should be practiced year-round. The Earth Day motto is, "Make Every Day Earth Day." Remember that even small changes make a difference. Your actions are important in keeping the earth healthy.

Safety Stickers

When cleaning up our planet, we should begin with our homes. In nature, bright red or orange coloring can be a warning to stay away. Some poisonous berries, snakes, and spiders bear bright markings for protection. Many things in our homes, such as cleaning products, paints, and polishes are poisonous. Make safety labels and place them on these products. The bright-colored labels will remind an adult to think before using them.

What You Will Need:

- masking tape or filing labels
- scissors
- markers or crayons

1. Cut tape or labels into 3-inch by 1-inch rectangles.

2. Use a red or bright colored marker to write a safety message. Here are some examples of warning words: Unsafe, Danger, Caution, Toxic, Hazard, Harmful, Stop.

3. Add a safety symbol, such as an X, a stop sign, a skull and crossbones, or a "yuck" face.

4. **Go on a safety hunt with an adult throughout your home.** Locate products in each room that could be harmful to you, your family, and your friends. Mark these items with Safety Stickers.

Get some filing labels . . .

DANGER

Use crayons or markers to write the warnings . . .

Stop

STOP

TOXIC

TOXIC

UNSAFE

DANGER

Place the finished warning labels throughout your house!

Earth Day Smarts:

If you cannot finish a glass of water, use the rest to water plants.

Dinner Dot-to-Dot

Do you know where your food comes from? Make a Dinner Dot-to-Dot to find out. You will create a foodshed. A foodshed is the path of your food supply. It shows the path the food you eat travels from where it is grown to where it is eaten.

What You Will Need:

- paper
- pencil
- map of the United States and/or the world
- dot stickers or reinforcement circles
- markers

1. Make a list of all the items you eat or drink during a meal.

2. Look on the packages of the food products that were used to prepare the meal. Read the labels carefully. Find out where each item has been grown, manufactured, or distributed.

3. Trace the map on page 26, ask an adult to make a copy, or print out a map from the Web site listed on page 31. Place a sticker on the map near the state or town that you live in.

4. Next, place stickers on the map near the state or town where the foods you eat are grown. Draw lines from your home sticker to the other stickers.

5. That is your foodshed. How far across the United States or the globe does your foodshed extend?

Start with a list
of foods . . .

1. orange juice
2. baked potato
3. carrots
4. beef
5. strawberries
6. whipped cream
7. pineapple chunks

Mark the state
where you are
from . . .

Locate the states where the
food you have eaten has
come from!

Earth Day Smarts:

Buy from local farms and
businesses.

Junk Journal

Recycled books and paper make great journals where you can write down your thoughts. Use old hardcover books with missing or torn pages that you planned on recycling.

What You Will Need:

- old hardcover picture book
- scissors
- paper used on one side only
- staples
- glue
- ribbon (optional)

1. Remove the pages from an old picture book with the spine still intact. Ask permission from an adult before you take apart any book!

2. Stack used paper so that the unused side is facing forward.

3. Use scissors to cut the paper stack so that it fits inside the book.

4. Staple the pages together on the left side.

5. Glue the bottom of the paper stack directly onto the inside of the book.

6. If you wish, cover the staples by gluing a length of ribbon on top of them.

Safety Note: Be sure to ask for help from an adult, if needed, to complete these crafts!

Remove the pages from an old book . . .

Staple together blank paper . . .

Glue the blank paper into the book . . .

Your journal is ready for you to use!

Earth Day Smarts:

Reuse giftwrap to cover your schoolbooks.

Mini Matchbook

Recycled paper and empty matchbooks combine to make a practical pocket-sized journal. Take your Mini Matchbook with you on your next hike or nature walk. Record what you see and hear. Mini Matchbooks also make eco-friendly gifts.

What You Will Need:

- empty matchbook
- ruler
- scissors

- paper used on one side only
- staples
- glue (optional)

1. Ask an adult for an empty matchbook. Remove the staples holding the match stubs to the matchbook cover.

2. With a ruler, measure the length and width of the inside of the matchbook. Use scissors to trim the used paper to match these dimensions.

3. Stack the trimmed paper so the unused side is facing forward.

4. Tuck the trimmed pages inside the pocket made by the bottom flap of the matchbook cover. Do not over fill. Staple the pages to the matchbook cover. You will staple from the bottom flap through to the back of the matchbook cover.

5. If you wish, glue the bottom of the paper stack directly onto the inside bottom of the matchbook.

Safety Note: Be sure to ask for help from an adult, if needed, to complete these crafts!

Remove the match stubs from the book . . .

Carefully cut out small pieces of paper . . .

Staple them into place . . .

EARTH DAY BOOK

Decorate the outside and you are finished!

Earth Day Smarts:

Turn off the lights when you leave a room.

Bounce Back Ball

This simple recycled toy is made from a product you see every day—rubber! Drying the sap of tropical trees makes rubber. Think about all of the things we use every day that are made from plants and trees.

What You Will Need:

- rubber bands

1. Collect rubber bands from toys, food, and other packaged products. The more rubber bands you have the bigger your ball will be.

2. Find two rubber bands of equal length. Cross one over the other in an X-shape.

3. Fold the rubber bands in half.

4. One at a time, tightly wrap the remaining rubber bands around the folded ones.

5. Use the ball for games—it really bounces! It also makes a colorful paperweight.

6. Add to your ball as you collect more rubber bands. Or remove rubber bands as needed for use in other projects.

Gather up lots of
rubber bands . . .

Start to build
your ball . . .

Make your ball as big
as you want!

Earth Day Smarts:
Use empty coffee cans to hold
pens, crayons, or coins.

Trash People

Since 1996, a German artist named H. A. Schult has built one thousand trash people. His life-size trash figures are made from aluminum cans, hard plastics, and other garbage that will not rot or break down easily. Mr. Shult photographs his army of trash people near famous world monuments such as the Great Pyramids in Egypt. Through his art, he hopes people will learn about the problems caused by garbage dumps and landfills. Make your own trash person using recyclable items or items you have around your house.

What You Will Need:

- half-gallon milk or juice container
- paint
- pipe cleaners
- buttons
- glue or strong tape

1. Thoroughly wash and dry an empty half-gallon milk or juice container. Standing upright, use the slanted side as your trash person's head.

2. Use your imagination to add eyes, a nose, hair, and other facial details.

3. Display your trash person atop dumpsters and lidded garbage cans on Earth Day.

Safety Note: Be sure to ask for help from an adult, if needed, to complete these crafts!

Start with a carton . . .

Gather up your supplies . . .

Use paint, pipe cleaners, and buttons for some of the details!

Cold MILK

CALCIUM

SHAKE WELL & BUY OFTEN

Earth Day Smarts:

The average person in the United States produces six and a half pounds of trash daily.

Extinction Game

There are over 1,300 endangered and threatened species in the United States. Unless we protect their habitats, these plants and animals may die out or become extinct. Once they have died out, they will never be seen on our planet again. The loss may affect other plants or animals who used them for food or shelter. Play the Extinction Game and think about how all of earth's species are interconnected.

What You Will Need:

- spring-type clothespins
- markers
- paper
- scissors
- crayons or markers

1. Use markers to write the names of endangered plants and animals on the clothespins. List one endangered species per clothespin. If you wish, decorate the clothespins to look like the endangered plant or animal. To help you get started, patterns for some of the animals can be found on page 27.

2. Make at least twenty-one clothespins. For three or more players, you may want to use more clothespins, in multiples of three.

3. For directions on how to play, go to page 28.

Start with a few
clothes pins . . .

Gather your art
supplies . . .

Decorate the playing
pieces . . .

Your game is
ready to play!

Earth Day Smarts:

In 1973, the Endangered
Species Act was passed to
help endangered animals.

RESPECT THE EARTH

Slick Water Wearable

Harmful wastes from homes, farms, and factories can pollute our water supply making it unsafe for humans and animals. When oil is spilled into rivers and oceans, it stays on the surface. It coats the feathers and fur of sea birds and mammals. Wear your Slick Water Wearable to show your awareness of the need for clean water.

What You Will Need:

- clear plastic pill bottle or empty glitter bottle
- vegetable oil
- food coloring
- glue
- string or ribbon
- glitter (optional)
- foil (optional)
- markers (optional)

1. Remove the label from an empty clear plastic pill bottle. Fill the bottle 2/3 full with water and 1/3 vegetable oil.

2. Add two drops of blue or green food coloring. If you wish, sprinkle glitter into the bottle. Cut or tear foil into small fish shapes. Add them to the bottle as well.

3. Squirt glue on the inside edge of the cap. Screw the cap onto the bottle. The glue should form an airtight seal once it is dry.

4. Tie string or ribbon around the cap edge. Wear as you would a necklace.

Safety Note: Be sure to ask for help from an adult, if needed, to complete these crafts!

Start with a small
clear bottle . . .

Add food coloring . . .

Add glitter and tin
foil. Tie a ribbon
around the bottle . . .

Make enough for
your family and
friends!

Earth Day Smarts:

You can save gallons of
water by turning off the
water when brushing your
teeth.

Greenbelt Planner Project

Undeveloped land surrounding a city is called a greenbelt. Greenbelts provide homes and food for animals and beauty and fresh air for humans. One way to protect our environment is to rethink how we plan cities. Pretend to be a city planner and design a city with a large greenbelt that can be enjoyed by all.

What You Will Need:

- poster board
- green tempera paint
- paintbrushes
- small boxes such as jewelry boxes, tea boxes, toothpick boxes
- construction paper
- tape
- markers

1. Use green tempera paint to paint the poster board. You may also use a piece of cardboard. While the paint is drying, think about your own town or city. What types of buildings might you find? Decide which types of buildings you want in your pretend community.

2. Collect small boxes. These will be the buildings. Cover the boxes with construction paper, grocery bag paper, or scrap paper. Use markers to draw in windows, doors, store signs, and house numbers.

3. Spend time arranging and rearranging the homes and buildings on the poster board. Try to arrange your Green City so that you have as much green space left on the board as possible.

4. When you have found the best arrangement, trace the bottoms of the buildings onto the board with a dark marker so that you can place them in the same spot the next time you play. Label each traced spot with the name of the building that belongs there. Keep track of how much green space you lose with each new addition.

Start with a piece of cardboard and small boxes . . .

Paint the boxes to be the buildings in your town . . .

Plan out your town . . .

Put the buildings in their places and your town is done!

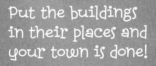

Earth Day Smarts:

With the help of an adult, organize a clean up day in your school or neighborhood.

23

Car Pool Game

To pool something is to share it. When people form a car pool, they share car rides. Car pools are a great way to reduce traffic and air pollution. As you play the Car Pool Game, think of things you can share with your friends.

What You Will Need:

- ⌾• empty tissue box
- ⌾• felt
- ⌾• glue
- ⌾• markers
- ⌾• buttons or bottle caps
- ⌾• deck of playing cards

1. Decorate the empty tissue box to look like a vehicle. You might add button wheels and foil for a windshield.

2. Collect buttons and bottle caps. You will need about twenty-five buttons or caps per player. Buttons or caps are each player's "pool." They represent people in a car pool. The object is to have the most people in your car pool at the end of the game.

3. For directions on how to play, go to page 29.

Start with a tissue box . . .

Decorate the box to look like a bus or car . . .

Begin the card game . . .

The player with the most buttons in the end wins!

Earth Day Smarts:

Use old clothes to make pillows for your room. Ask an adult to help.

Patterns

Use tracing paper to copy the patterns on these pages. Ask an adult to help you cut and trace the shapes onto construction paper.

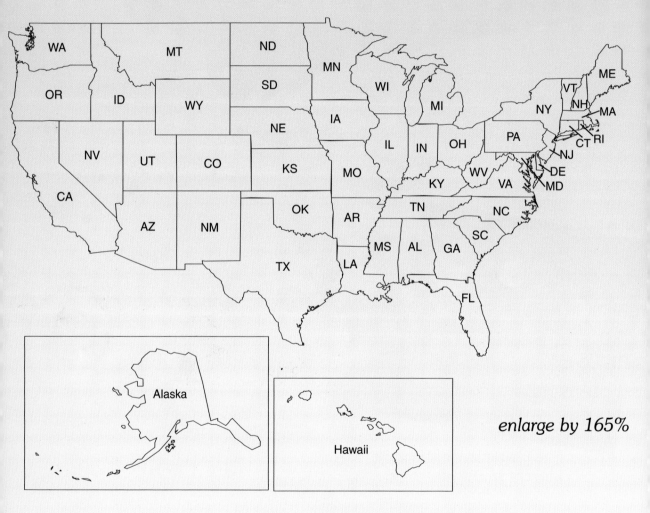

enlarge by 165%

Safety Note: Be sure to ask for help from an adult, if needed, to complete these crafts!

enlarge by 170%

27

Game Rules

To Play the Extinction Game

1. Divide the clothespins equally among two or more players.

2. The first player begins by placing a row of three clothespins on a level surface. Space the clothespins so that they are parallel to one another yet not touching.

3. The second player then sets three clothespins on top of the first row so they are perpendicular to the first row of clothespins.

4. Continue in this manner until all remaining clothespins are stacked on top of each other.

5. Players will now take turns carefully removing a clothespin from the middle of the stack. You may not remove them from the top until the very end of the round.

6. When the stack collapses, the player must take all the clothespins that have fallen.

7. Once all of the pins are removed, the player with the least endangered species wins.

To Play the Car Pool Game

1. Place four buttons inside the car.

2. Play the Car Pool Game like the card game "War."

3. Remove face cards from the deck. Shuffle the playing cards and deal them out to all players until no cards remain.

4. Each player then stacks his or her cards face down in a pile. During each round, players reveal the top card in his or her pile.

5. The player with the highest card wins that round. He or she does not remove any buttons from his or her pool.

6. Players who lost the round must place buttons from their pool into the vehicle. Each losing player will remove a different amount from his or her pool. The amount of buttons removed is the number of the highest card in the round minus the number on the cards other players have drawn. For example, if the winning card that round was an eight and your card was a six, you would take two buttons from your pool and place it inside the vehicle. If your card was a four, you would place four buttons inside the vehicle.

7. If two players flip over the same number—such as two fives or two sevens, both may take two buttons from inside the car.

8. Play until all of the cards have been flipped over or until one player runs out of buttons. The player with the most buttons wins the game.

Reading About Earth Day

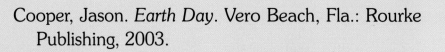

Cooper, Jason. *Earth Day*. Vero Beach, Fla.: Rourke Publishing, 2003.

Landau, Elaine. *Earth Day: Keeping Our Planet Clean*. Berkeley Heights, N.J.: Enslow Publishers, Inc., 2002.

Lowery, Linda. *Earth Day*. Minneapolis, Minn.: Carolrhoda Books, 2004.

Pfiffner, George. *Earth-Friendly Holidays: How to Make Fabulous Gifts and Decorations From Reusable Objects*. New York: Wiley, 1995.

Roop, Connie, and Peter Roop. *Let's Celebrate Earth Day*. Brookfield, Conn.: Millbrook Press, 2001.

Ross, Kathy. *Every Day is Earth Day: A Craft Book*. Brookfield, Conn.: Millbrook Press, 1995.

Celebrate Earth Day—Every Day

Find out more about Earth Day.

<http://www.kidsdomain.com/holiday/earthday>

Earth Day Crafts and Projects

This site from Enchanted Learning has crafts and projects about Earth Day.

<http://www.enchantedlearning.com/crafts/
earthday/>

Kids Corner: Endangered Species

Learn more about endangered species at this site from the U.S. Fish and Wildlife Service.

<http://endangered.fws.gov/kids/index.html>

Outline Map: USA with State Borders

Use this map for the Dinner Dot-to-Dot.

<http://www.enchantedlearning.com/usa/
outlinemaps/states50/>

Index